Patric

C000245212

The Poems of Jules Laforgue

Patrick Caulfield
The Poems of Jules Laforgue

Arts Council
Collection

A National Touring Exhibition organised by the Hayward Gallery for the
Arts Council of England

Exhibition organised by Ann Jones
Assisted by Elena Lukaszewicz

Patrick Caulfield's screenprints: photographs by John Webb
Patrick Caulfield: photograph © Guglielmo Galvin
Franz Skarbina *Portrait of Jules Laforgue* 1885: photograph © Harlingue-Viollet

Catalogue designed by Andrew Johnson

Printed by Balding + Mansell

Cover: Plate 22 *My life inspires so many desires!*

The screenprints and poems are reproduced by kind permission of the artist and the publisher,
and were originally published in *Some poems of Jules Laforgue with images by Patrick Caulfield*
© Patrick Caulfield and Petersburg Press 1973 All Rights Reserved

The publishers have made every effort to contact all copyright holders. If proper acknowledgement
has not been made, we ask copyright holders to contact us

ISBN 1 85332 141 9

Arts Council Collection, National Touring and Hayward Gallery exhibition catalogues are distributed by
Cornerhouse Publications, 70 Oxford Street, Manchester M1 5NH (tel. 0161 237 9662; fax. 0161 237 9664)

Arts Council Collection

The Arts Council Collection is the largest national loan collection of post-war British art. Its works are loaned on a temporary basis to exhibitions and longer-term to museums and public buildings. The Collection also forms an integral part of the National Touring Exhibitions service which, from its base at the Hayward Gallery, on the South Bank in London, enables art to be seen throughout the UK. The Collection is administered by the Hayward Gallery for the Arts Council of England.

Isobel Johnstone, *Curator*

Preface

Some poems of Jules Laforgue with images by Patrick Caulfield was published by Petersburg Press in 1973 and, in the following year, the Arts Council Collection acquired a copy of this limited edition book. Caulfield's brilliant colours, characteristic black outlines and quality of printing make this one of the most vivid artists' publications of recent years. The screenprints are complementary images, rather than illustrations in the usual sense, with the melancholy atmosphere of Caulfield's interiors finding a direct equivalent in Laforgue's poetry.

This is the latest in a series of small-scale exhibitions concerned with artists' illustrations for poetry and prose texts, and we are delighted that it will begin its nation-wide tour in July at the National Literature Centre in Swansea. Appropriately, the poet Sean O'Brien has written the introductory essay. We are grateful to him for his illuminating text, which explores the work of Laforgue and examines the ways in which Caulfield has successfully translated the written word into evocative visual statements. Finally, we would very much like to thank Patrick Caulfield himself for his enthusiasm for the project.

Henry Meyric Hughes,
Director of Exhibitions
Ann Jones,
Exhibition Organiser

Patrick Caulfield on Jules Laforgue

I was introduced to Laforgue's poetry by a fellow student at the Royal College of Art in about 1962. He had borrowed a translation from the college library and thought I would like it. I did. It seemed wonderfully concise, managing to be both romantic and ironic. I returned the book to the library a long time late. A rather selfish act.

Laforgue was my natural choice when I was invited to do a limited edition book. The images I produced are complementary images, not illustrations. Some of the connections are a bit tenuous, others are obvious. I tried to imagine what Laforgue might have been looking at when he thought of the poems, knowing, of course, that certain of the images are totally of another period to Laforgue's lifetime: poetic licence with poetic licence.

A Week of Sundays:
Jules Laforgue and Patrick Caulfield

Forty years ago, Kingsley Amis remarked that 'nobody wants any more poems about paintings'. In fact, whether wanted or not, poems about paintings were much in evidence among Amis's contemporaries and have greatly proliferated in the intervening decades. The list of distinguished poets who have found stimulus in visual art would be a long one. It is rather more difficult for a poet to assess the extent to which the process can be found working in the opposite direction, with painters pursuing suggestions from poetry, though a notable example is David Hockney's 'Blue Guitar' series of etchings (1976–77), which refers to both Wallace Stevens and Pablo Picasso. In this area, the work of Hockney's contemporary, Patrick Caulfield, is of equal interest.

Aside from the pleasures of finding Caulfield's images juxtaposed with the poems of Jules Laforgue, the bold, deliberate outlines of Caulfield's pictures, with their equally bold colourings, which work both to isolate objects from the surrounding world and to emphasize their status as *things* – a fallen cigarette, a bedside lamp, a clock, the elaborate ironwork of a balcony – remind us of the often maddeningly sedate and even inert world from which Laforgue's ironic rhapsodies of unstable identity actually arise. Caulfield's elegant and witty pictures are not illustrations, but they are evidence of his understanding of both the charm and distress Laforgue transmits for his readers.

Jules Laforgue was born in Montevideo but largely brought up in France. Among the major factors shaping his brief but remarkable career was his surprising failure to get into university. Influential friends then secured him the post of Reader to the Francophile Empress Augusta

at the German court, and Laforgue spent the next five years travelling with the court to various locations including Berlin, as well as the Rhine city of Koblenz, and Baden-Baden. For Laforgue, the famous spa of Baden-Baden offered limitless boredom, frustration and futility. He spent his time writing, or engaging in erotic dithering with ladies of the court, to the accompaniment of the relentless bleatings of the town band. The experience was evidently a powerful stimulus towards the innovations of tone, attitude and method which have proved so enduringly influential on English-speaking poets since T.S. Eliot first drew attention to Laforgue's work.

Perhaps equally important for Laforgue was his interest in art criticism, in which he had a growing reputation in Paris by the time of his early death from tuberculosis. He was quick to understand and advocate Impressionism, and although it would be unhelpful to call him an Impressionist poet, he seems to have sensed a strong analogy between the dynamic anti-academicism of the Impressionists and his own efforts to render dramatically the experience of consciousness.

As with any poet, isolated description of technical preoccupations – it is to Laforgue, really, that we owe free verse – can fail to convey the real climate of the work. Laforgue is a poet of horror and hilarity, passion and impossibility, romance, irony and crippling ennui, of the large statement cut off at the knees by wit and yet still needing, somehow, to be made. His characteristic juxtaposition or blending of high and low styles has become part of the customary language of modern poetry, so ingrained as often to be barely noticeable.

The multiple ambiguity of Laforgue's poems and his pointed use of rhyme make translation even more of a challenge than usual. For English readers, the most familiar translation of his work may be the late Martin Bell's *Winter Coming On* (*L'Hiver Qui Vient*), which finds some English equivalents for the poem's mood. Patrick Caulfield's pictures refer to lines from translations by Patricia Terry published by the University of California Press in 1958. These (like Peter Dale's more recent versions) work hard to convey the endemic duplicity of Laforgue's tone:

In this distant cliff-bound village, towards the bells

Once again I come down, through the piercing stares

Of children out for blessings on tepid rolls;

And then, at home, my wretched heart despairs.

The old roofs' sparrows chirping at my window

Watch me eat, without appetite, à la carte . . .

Complaint about a certain Sunday

Laforgue's letters reveal an outrageously witty man, ever alert to the comedy of circumstances, and Caulfield's image of the menu exhibits a similar appreciation – bare, banal, insistently itself, wholly unresponsive to the scale and disorder of the feelings the poet seeks to dramatize.

The contrast between internal near-hysteria and outward repose receives a further, somewhat chilling re-creation in Caulfield's image for a line from *Sundays* (the week seems to have been all Sundays for Laforgue). The poem as a whole paces about in the prison of erotic failure and inhibition, and 'You'll be sick if you spend all your time indoors' is its lowest, funniest point. Caulfield uses a typical feature of German decoration – the heart-shaped spyhole in a wooden wall or fence – but he complicates the glaring sentimentality of the image by his use of colour, applying the green of nature to an interior from which the sky beyond seems quite inaccessible, so that the location of 'indoors' seems to be the mind itself, a condition with no outdoors to escape to.

Recurrent in Laforgue's work is a sense of the speaker possessing energy without the power to apply it in order to wrest control of experience. His early concern with the influence of a pre-Freudian Unconscious or Fate can be seen as an attempt to give coherence to a habitual experience of the absurd. Something like this seems to underlie *Pierrots* (one of several Pierrot poems), where the line which has caught Caulfield's interest is the

last of the second stanza, which takes place after a row with a woman:

You should have seen me after that argument!

I wandered about in the cruellest kind of torment

Crying to the walls: My God! My God! Will she relent?

The accompanying image is of a clock of the most unadorned and modern kind, suspended in a jaundiced institutional yellow. It looks both implacable and ridiculous, an object to which a lover in terror of rejection might well pay constant homage, yet one quite empty in itself, like nearly all the images Caulfield finds in Laforgue. Although we may think of Laforgue as a precursor of the great mass of image-rich modern poetry, he is not himself so much an artist of the visible as a reader of its connotations. The poems are, for example, full of an aimless but necessary promenading in the streets of towns and cities in preparation for some even less satisfactory idleness to follow. Equally, they are full of overheard music, or reminders of things not present. The visible world is continually supplanted by its associations. Paradoxically, this may make the poems inviting and accessible to the visual artist.

Laforgue's sidelong, glancing, distracted atmosphere, whose extreme self-consciousness has no adequate object on which to settle, seems to become a structural feature of several of Caulfield's pictures. He comes at things from an angle – the wall with its spyhole, the trellis, the railings on a balcony and in a street, the curved railing over a pool, the windows. This approach, usually seeming to work from the left and upwards to the right, makes the pictures' contents the focus of an intense attention which is, none the less, seeking something more, which should, but never can, be found beyond them. As a visual correlative, this would be hard to better. Instead of the more obvious visual language which could be derived from Laforgue's habitual inclusion of girls in white dresses, eyes, water, sun, moon and so on, Caulfield takes on a much emptier frame, with few of the obvious symbolic properties used by the poems. Full of objects intended for human use, the pictures contain not a single human figure, and suggest an unbreakable solitude. Perhaps the most eloquent of these is the lamp, which accompanies the line 'I've only the friendship of hotel rooms', from *Solo by moonlight*, one of the great series of *Last Poems*, where Laforgue's technique and attitude seem wholly unified. Here the poet (or one of him), riding on the roof of a swaying stagecoach, reads his romantic loss into the journey through the night. The mood manages to be both despairing and exultant: the lover relishes his loss since he cannot relish the beloved. Laforgue,

who departed from Berlin on the
day the Imperial Palace on Unter
den Linden first received electric
light, might have been amused by
the challenge presented by Caulfield's
image of the bedside lamp. Clearly
one of a million found in a million
rooms, its function is to illuminate
a solitude which may be everywhere
the same but must, however, be
suffered in individual isolation:

Let's accumulate irreparables!

Do better than our fate!

**The stars are more numerous
than the sand**

**Of seas where others have seen
her body bathe;**

But all to Death will report.

And there's no port . . .

Sean O'Brien

Biographical note
Sean O'Brien is a poet, critic, editor and
broadcaster. His fourth book of poems,
Ghost Train, will be published by
Oxford University Press in 1995, and a
selection of his earlier work will appear
in *Penguin Modern Poets 5*.

Poems and Plates

Complaint
About a lady good and dead

She fled along the avenue;
I followed, magnetized!
Her eyes were saying, 'Alas, I knew
You recognized me too!'

I followed, magnetized!
Ingenuous mouth, regretful eyes;
Oh, why did I recognize
That loyal dream of you?

Lips so pure, but old her eyes;
A white carnation veined too blue!
Oh, nothing, of course, but a stillborn prize,
Far too dead to be true.

Sleep, carnation veined too blue,
Human life somehow survives
Without, defunct now, you.
I'll fast at home for this surprise!

True, she was no one I knew.

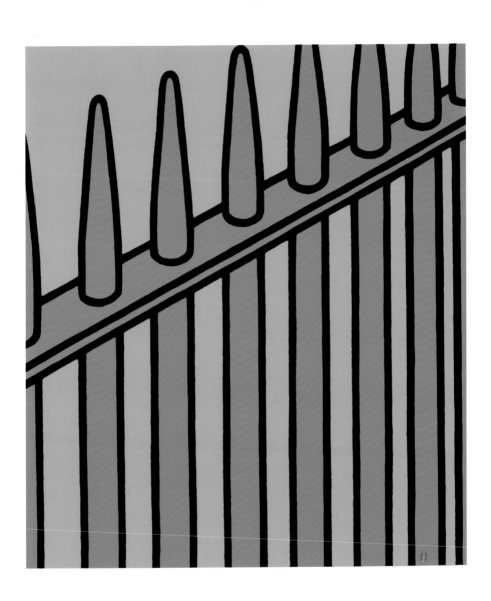

Plate 3 **19**

Complaint
About a certain Sunday

Man isn't really so bad, nor woman ephemeral.
Ah! fools cooling your heels at the casino,
All men weep one day, and every woman's maternal;
Everything's filial, you know!
It's only that Fates employ such sorry prejudice
To make us, far and separate, self-exiles,
And blindly calling each other egotists,
And worn out with looking for some unique Anodyne.
Ah! until nature has pity on us,
I'll take my life monotonous.

In this distant cliff-bound village, towards the bells
Once again I come down, through the piercing stares
Of children out for blessings on tepid rolls;
And then, at home, my wretched heart despairs.
The old roofs' sparrows chirping at my window
Watch me eat, without appetite, à la carte;
Perhaps they house my dead friends' souls?
I throw them some bread; as if wounded, they depart!
Ah! until nature has pity on us,
I'll take my life monotonous.

She left yesterday. Perhaps I mind?
Ah yes! So that's what hurts!

Plate 4   **21**

My life is caught among your faithful skirts!
Her handkerchief swept me along the Rhine . . .
Alone. — The Sunset holds back its Quadriga's prancing
In rays where the midges' ballet is dancing,
Then, toward the soup-smoking roofs, he complains . . .

And Evening so elusively explains . . .
Ah! until nature has pity on us,
Must life be so monotonous?
Fans, pointed arches, or for incest — how many eyes,
Since Being first had hopes, demand their rights!
O skies, will the eyes decay like the rest?
Oh, alone! alone! and so cold!
How many Fall afternoons can life digest?
Ennui, cold eunuch, wallows in our dreams!
So, since we'll never be madrepores again,
We'd better console each other, my fellow men.
And, until nature has pity on us,
Let's try to live monotonous.

Plate 16   **23**

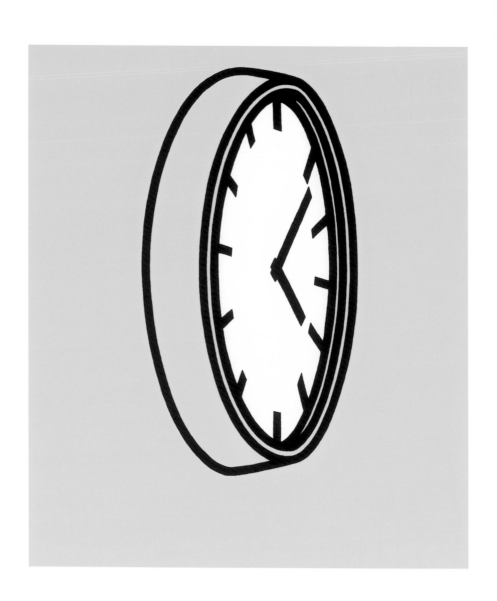

Plate 8   25

Plate 15 **27**

The coming winter

Sentimental Blockade! Express from the rising Sun! . . .
Oh! falling rain, oh! nightfall,
Oh! the wind . . .
All Saints' Day, Christmas, the New Year,
Oh, in the drizzle, all my fine chimneys! . . .
Of factories . . .

There's nowhere to sit down, all the benches are wet;
Believe me, it's all over once again,
All the benches are wet, the woods are so rusty,
And so many horns have sounded ton ton, have
sounded ton taine! . . .

Ah! storm clouds rushed from the Channel coasts,
You can boast of spoiling the last of our Sundays.

Drizzle;
In the wet fields, the spiderwebs
Give way to the waterdrops, and fizzle.
Plenipotentiary suns of blond river gold-mines,
Or agricultural pantomimes,
Where is your tomb?
This evening a worn-out sun lies dead on top of the hill,
Lies on his side, in the broom, on his coat.
A sun white as tavern spit

On a litter of golden broom,
The yellow autumnal broom.
And the horns resound!
Calling him . . .
Calling him back to himself!

Taiaut! Taiaut! and hallali!
O doleful anthem, when will you die! . . .
And madly they have fun . . .
And he lies there like a gland torn from a neck,
Shivering, without anyone! . . .

On, on, and hallali!
In the lead is Winter, that's understood;
Oh! the turns in the highways,
And without the wandering Little Red Riding Hood! . . .
Oh! their ruts from last month's cars,
Trails in a Don Quixotic climb
Toward the routed cloud patrols
That the wind mauls toward transatlantic folds! . . .
Accelerate, accelerate, it's the well-known season, this time.

And the wind, last night, really put on a show!
O havoc, O nests, O diffident gardens!
My heart and my sleep: O echoes of axe-blows!

All those branches had their green leaves still,
Now the underbrush, only a mulch of dead leaves;
Leaves, leaflets, may a good wind's will
Race you off in swarms toward ponds,
Or for the game warden's fireplace,
Or for ambulance mattresses
For soldiers far away from France.

Plate 20   **31**

It's the season, the season; rust invades the masses,
Rust gnaws the kilometric spleens
Of telegraph wires on highways no one passes.

The horns, the horns, the horns — melancholy! . . .
Melancholy! . . .

Go away, changing their tone,
Changing their tone and their tune,
Ton ton, ton taine, ton ton! . . .
The horns, the horns, the horns! . . .
Have gone away to the North Wind.

I can't get out of this echoing tone . . .
It's the season, the season, farewell grape harvests! . . .
Now, with a patience of angels, come the rains;
Farewell harvests, baskets, nothing remains,
Those Watteau twig-baskets under the chestnut trees.
It's the cough in dormitories coming back,
Nursed by only a stranger's herbal tea,
The neighbourhood sadness of pulmonary phthisis,
And all the metropolitan wretchedness.

But wool clothes, rubbers, pharmacies, dreams,
Curtains drawn back from balconies of shores
Facing the sea of suburban roofs,
Prints, lamps, cakes and tea,
Won't I have only you to love! . . .
(Oh! and then, do you know, apart from the pianos,
Each week, austere twilight mystery,
The journalistic
Vital statistics?)

No, no! it's the season; the planet repines!
May the storm, the storm
Unravel the slippers knitted by Time!
It's the season, O rendings! the season!
And every year, every year
I'll try in chorus to sound its rhyme.

Poems and Plates

The twenty-two images illustrating twelve poems were prepared as studies for original screenprints by Patrick Caulfield between 1969 and 1972. Colour proofing took place in London at the studios of Christopher Betambeau in 1971–72, and the editions were printed on Neobond synthetic paper in Stuttgart in 1972. The poetry text was set in Futura Bold to the typographical layout of Eric Ayers as agreed by Patrick Caulfield. The book was published in three editions of 200, 200 and 100 impressions by the Petersburg Press in association with Waddington Galleries in 1973. All the works measure 40.5 x 35.5 cm, height before width.

Complaint about certain annoyances

1 *Ah! this Life is so everyday*

Complaint about a certain Sunday

2 *Watch me eat, without appetite, à la carte*

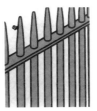

Complaint about a lady good and dead

3 *She fled along the avenue*

Complaint about a certain Sunday

4 *Her handkerchief swept me along the Rhine*
5 *I'll take my life monotonous*

Sundays

6 *You'll be sick if you spend all your time indoors*

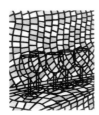

Pierrots

7 *Crying to the walls: My God! My God! Will she relent?*
8 *All these confessions ...*

Pierrot Phrases

9 *Making circles on park lagoons*

 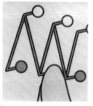

Derniers vers IX

10 *Oh! if one of Them, some fine evening, would try*
11 *Thus she would come, escaped, half-dead to my door*

Another complaint of Lord Pierrot

12 *And, with my eyes bolting toward the Unconscious*

Complaint about certain annoyances

13 *We wanted to bleed the Silence*

Complaint concerning melancholy and literary debates

14 *Along a twilighted sky*
15 *Oh Helen, I roam my room*

Solo by moonlight

16 *I've only the friendship of hotel rooms*
17 *She'll have forgotten her scarf*

About a defunct lady

18 *And I am alone in my house*

The coming winter

19 *All the benches are wet, the woods are so rusty*

20 *Ah! storm clouds rushed from the Channel coasts*

21 *Curtains drawn back from balconies of shores*

Complaint concerning melancholy and literary debates

22 *My life inspires so many desires!*

Patricia Terry's English translations of the poems were first published by the University of California Press in 1958 and subsequently in *Some poems of Jules Laforgue with images by Patrick Caulfield*, Petersburg Press, 1973.

Patrick Caulfield

Patrick Caulfield was born in London on 29 January 1936. He studied at
Chelsea School of Art from 1956 to 1960 and returned there to teach from
1963 to 1971. He spent the intervening years at the Royal College of Art,
where he was a contemporary of David Hockney, R.B. Kitaj and Allen Jones.
He became connected with this generation of Pop artists, although his work
was very different in style from his contemporaries. At this time, he expressed
a great admiration for the work of Léger and Gris and developed a style
using bright flat colours outlined with a contrasting tone. He has frequently
chosen the traditional subject matter of still life and interiors for his work,
but has interpreted them in a totally modern way. He has made screenprints
regularly since the mid-1960s and they complement his activities as a painter
with their bold use of colour and line.

In 1984 he was commissioned to design the sets and costumes for Michael
Corder's new ballet *Party Games* at the Royal Opera House and in 1995 he
designed the set and costumes for *Rhapsody* by Frederick Ashton, also at the
Royal Opera House. In 1986 he selected the exhibition *The Artist's Eye* at
the National Gallery in London.

He has exhibited widely since the mid-1960s and his one-man shows include:
Scottish Arts Council Gallery, Edinburgh (1975); Tortue Gallery, Santa
Monica, California (1977); Walker Art Gallery, Liverpool/Tate Gallery,
London (1981); Nishimura Gallery, Tokyo (1982); Arnolfini Gallery, Bristol
(1983); National Museum of Fine Art, Rio de Janeiro/British Council tour
(1985–87); Serpentine Gallery, London (1992); as well as regular exhibitions
at Waddington Galleries since the late 1960s.

Patrick Caulfield lives and works in London.

Jules Laforgue

Jules Laforgue was born on 16 August 1860 in Montevideo, Uruguay, where his father taught French. The second son in a family of eleven, he was educated at Tarbes in the Pyrenees. He moved to Paris in 1876, where he developed a strong interest in painting and wrote a pioneering essay on Impressionism. In 1881, he was appointed Reader to the German Empress Augusta and moved to Berlin where he spent the next five years. In 1886, he married an English governess, Leah Lee, who had taught him English in Berlin, and the couple moved to Paris. There, however, they lived in poverty, and Laforgue died from tuberculosis on 20 August 1887, aged only twenty-seven. His wife died of the same disease, ten months later.

His first book of poems, *Les Complaintes* was published in 1885, and *Moralités Légendaires* was published shortly after his death. His poetry, combining symbolism and impressionism, reflected modern city life at the time and was an important influence on Alain-Fournier, T.S. Eliot and Ezra Pound. Laforgue is still admired for his fresh expression, innovative handling of free verse and inventive rhymes. He was also known for his early protests in support of the emancipation of women.

Further Reading

Dale, Peter, 1986, *Poems of Jules Laforgue*, Anvil Press Poetry, London
Gilmour, Pat, 1979, *Understanding Prints. A Contemporary Guide*,
Waddington Galleries, London
Livingstone, Marco, 1981, *Patrick Caulfield, Paintings 1963–81*,
Tate Gallery, London
Livingstone, Marco, 'Patrick Caulfield Paintings 1963–1992' in *Art &
Design*, May–June 1992, vol.7, no. 5/6
Robertson, Bryan, 1981, *Patrick Caulfield. Prints 1964–81*,
Waddington Galleries, London